Tourniquet

© Copyright 2018 Vanessa Page

All poems included here are copyright to the author and no copies may be made in any manner whatsoever without first gaining written permission through the publisher.

Walleah Press
PO Box 368
North Hobart
Tasmania 7002 Australia
ralph.wessman@walleahpress.com.au

ISBN: 978-1-877010-88-0

Tourniquet

Vanessa Page

Poems

I. Arterial 1

Pink	2
Canary in the Coal Town	3
Papier Mache	4
Margaret Olley's Flannel Flowers	5
Christmas Day in Harlaxton	6
Summer Solstice	8
Like a Virgin	9
Mathinna	10
Timeshare	12
Farm Duties	13
The Instinct of Sharks	14
South Solitary	15
Terrarium	16
Home	17

II. Tourniquet 19

Wattlebird Pie	20
Aylan	21
Manus Island Love Poem	22
Bellarine Machines	24
Pristella Maxillaris	26
Break-up	27
Climbing Mount Yasur	28
Signs of Life	29
Homesick on the Plateau Mont-Royal	30
Balloon	31

Something Old, Something New	32
Toowoomba Carnival Queen	34
The Hazards #1	35
The Hazards #2	36
Evandale	37

III. Occlusion   39

Skin	40
A Remittance Man	41
Keilawarra	42
Fontanelle	43
Maranoa	44
Itinerant Damnation #1	45
Itinerant Damnation #2	46
The Torpey Spoon	47
The Mort Street Badlands	49
Petrichor	51
Tyenna: *What comes after extinction*	52
Back River	53
Soldier Trees	54
Inheritance	56

Vanessa Page was born in Toowoomba Queensland, and currently resides in Cashmere, north of Brisbane, Queensland.

She is the author of three collections of poetry, the chapbook *Feeding Paper Tigers* (2012, ALS Press), *Confessional Box* (2013, Walleah Press) and *China Bull* (2016, Work + Tumble), which was a collaborative work with John Koenig.

Confessional Box was the winner of the 2013 Anne Elder Award for the best first book of poetry.

Vanessa performs her poetry widely, and has performed at various events including the Queensland Poetry Festival, USQ Bookcase, SLQ Literary Salon, Couplet, the Nuyorican, New York and the Riverbend Poetry Series. She blogs at vanessapage.wordpress.com.

Poems in this collection have been previously published at *Cuttlefish*, *Cordite* (Obsolete, No Theme V, Explode, Silence and The End issues), *Island* (152), *Australian Poetry, Foam:e* (11), *Page Seventeen, Stilts, Grapple Annual, Australian Poetry Journal* (5.2 and 6.1), *Southerly* (Elemental issue), Pressure Gauge Press, *Writ Review, Sotto*, and *Dazzled* (ACU Poetry Prize Anthology).

Poems in this collection have also been short or long listed for the Ron Pretty Poetry Prize, the ACU Poetry Prize, the Tom Collins Poetry Prize and the University of Canberra Vice Chancellor's Prize.

'Christmas Day in Harlaxton' won the 2016 Martha Richardson Poetry Prize. 'Something Old, Something New' won the 2014 Martha Richardson Poetry Prize. 'Margaret Olley's Flannel Flowers' won the 2017 Henry Kendall Poetry Prize.

Chapter pages feature lyrics from:

'Lateralus', Tool – from the album 'Lateralus', 2002, written by Danny Carey, Justin Chancellor, Adam Jones, Maynard James Keenan, Volcano Entertainment, California, USA.

'Jesus Alone', Nick Cave and the Bad Seeds – from the album 'Skeleton Tree', 2016, written by Nick Cave, Bad Seed Ltd, Brighton, UK.

'Dickeye', Jerry Cantrell – from the album 'Boggy Depot', 1998, written by Jerry Cantrell, Columbia, California, USA.

Cover art by Jessica Fazakarley, Mondo Hue Designs

For Owen

I.
Arterial

Spiral out, keep going
Spiral out, keep going
Spiral out, keep going
Spiral out, keep going
Tool, Lateralus

For Trish Reid

Pink

Pink-puce the scar seamed skin where they opened her up: it was a long march between first nipple nubs   and mammogram pink, all going on for years before it was the colour to best represent breasts   all this time, a benign trap   the prettiest hue spreading quietly, widely   ripe for the taking: sugar baby, budding   sweet to taste, into femme: a girlie-babe – soft and (com)pliant   doll parts – the some times pink sometimes swollen submits to the bubblegum-full spectacle   popped by finger, but not the pinkie one   *what are ya? a girl or something*   that delicate integer lends itself to more ladylike pursuits   suits   standing erect, to attention – over bone china and strawberry jam – almost the shade of calendar blood, drip-drip-drip-dripping – a metronome-tether   *show us yer pink bits*   hem-length and décolletage   in the typing pool, the click of candy pink nails – adornment-cum-burden   it's how she lost touch in the first place, lost the skills to dig out, scrap through, build,   manage on her own   *can you help me with this dear?*   clack-clack stilettos   can't drive in those things   chivalry is control is chivalry   not immediately obvious   sitting alone, at the kitchen table, cutting out a dress pattern   something nice for herself – see how those pinking shears leave a neat, jagged cut   *nothing to see here*   damsel bait - in a framed photograph - in a pink satin puffy-sleeved number at her high school formal   flesh-flash   the little pills in little pink plastic shells in purses   overnight stays   *she said-she did -she wore-what?*   prise apart the teeth, suckling (help me) suckling   blue for the boys, pink for the girls: lacey crop-top bra and panties   glitter-bug   precedes heart-shaped box   precedes baby-pink lip gloss, cherry-pop   precedes pregnancy kit, precedes pink-ribbon swarms of women, precedes pink-puce the scar seamed skin where she was opened up – long after it was the colour to best   represent breasts.

Canary in the Coal Town

Somewhere provincial she stirs thin air. A sulphur-
yellow slash of tee-shirt daisies; pink knees and
elbows. As if shaken loose from the bomber's nest.

Her mother is at the bus shelter, sitting, counting out
last night's change – handbag heavy. Wearing pieces
of past unions around her fingers like shrapnel.

In the council-kept grass, a treacle-eyed dog sniffs
at something pale and still. This postcode – as obvious
as the saw-toothed bones, testing the length of its pelt.

Papier Mache

This spit-polished veneer has street appeal
and is open for inspection.
In these shutter-speed days, family portraits
bear the least resemblance to anything real,
paintbox-bright statements, all flourishes and filters
 – tumbling and spreading from the news feed's mouth.
It's the arrangement that is the most exhausting
– the nipping and tucking, the painstaking placement;
all that sure-footed running with the bulls.
What remains of her curls on the editing room floor,
as she exhales, stripped down to a wick –
hauling the dead weight of domestic bliss like a cadaver.
Down there, she traces the panic room's button
with her finger, as her audience chatters and twitters
with absent kindness – cutting her a break
in digital platitudes; the emptiest of intimacies.
It's a fragile masking agent, enough to hold the moon
at arm's length from the sleeping faces of her children;
keep the dark sirens, doll-faced and dead-eyed
from making their move – from clambering and twisting
their way out of her, as everything real is stuck,
fishbone-cruel at the back of her throat.
It's a complex deal to strike, and she wonders
how it came down to this – all this keeping up appearances
– all these papier mache strips
holding up this perfect, terrible mess.

Margaret Olley's Flannel Flowers

Pandanus trees rim a small beach, stagger-lurch-stuck at the back of
the dunes; prop-rooted trunks shouldering the weight of canopy fruit –

spiky aureole-crowns poking peep-holes in the weather. I'm passing
through someone else's country, feet-deep in the bright purple of pig-

face flowers, unhurried, coastal-cool, picking a path through the sand
sweep – alive with native morning glory and creeper-vines, thick with

squish-yellow flowers; each claiming the verges, resisting the spray of
salt – the constant shift of the ground beneath them. Mine is a country

of spinifex and brigalow – tin roofs reflecting the desolation of heat:
womal trees and gidyea, all following the slow brown run of the river.

Here, familiar is the tubular beauty of the banksia, the yolk-studded
fingers of coast-myall; the fleeting mimicry between the silver-backed

leaves and a gleaming catch of river perch: August sun setting a tin-foil
blaze on the Maranoa. This is not my country, but I'm looking through

its portholes, thinking of the Olley painting I cut out of a magazine
once – of the coastal flannel flowers: the way they spoke, perfectly wild

in a fluted cream jug, spilling and existing in no particular arrangement.
Effortlessly beautiful in the same way one's own country can be, and by

extension: the pockets of another – searching for white, star-shaped
faces beyond the sands, in the rippling dunes, in the shrubby headlands

bursting with strange botanicals – all of it, within and outside of myself.

Christmas Day in Harlaxton

On Christmas morning, the devil slips under the edge
of a green canvas marquee – another family tradition

to keep the festive underbelly from view. There's a
pecking order of men, propped on kitchen chairs –

dragged outside without ceremony. They squash the
bruise-yellow vinyl flat, sweat-patched and moustachioed

in ruggers and singlets and rubber thongs. The palette of
khaki, mustard and mud – everywhere, a regular truth in

the threat of sex and muscle. They eat first, a conga line
of patriarchs, peeling blackened bits off barbequed birds.

The plastic tub of tabouleh up-ended near the door: *we
don't want any of that fucking weirdo shit here.* The women

sigh, deep inside themselves. This is just another day to
'get through'. At the sink, a pot-bellied uncle grabs a niece

from behind. She starts, fresh-skinned inside a sleeveless
cotton shift – the rough two-step and lark just enough

to make nubile flesh. Downstairs, the kids run and
shriek in sarsaparilla-high notes. The eldest boy-cousin

barks orders from the top of the fence. The others
laugh and call him the King. Little girls bring offerings

on paper serviettes as the devil lurches off his stumps.
And before plum pudding even makes it out, one of

the piss-fuelled sons is shaping up to the old man. They
shake the earth like diprotodons beside the hills-hoist.

Hate-faced and cussing, their fists in knots of flesh and
rage. The in-law from the city waits it out – keeps his

blonde-headed girls away from their grandfather's lap.
When Boxing Day dawns, there will be nothing left

for the sun to beat to a pulp. They'll sleep it all off.
Wives and aunts will unpack the same old excuses.

Summer Solstice

Mango trees
wear fruit bling
like two-bit hookers

top-shelf drunk
backs turned
on the lawn

lorikeets
arrive like rain
tearing at the pulp

a sweet rot
rises in this
sex-sweat heat.

Like a Virgin

Dolled up in pleated white frocks and veils for Jesus
– all the little girls groomed in stiff new shoes and dusty-satin

communion trappings, handed down from cousin-to-cousin.
Standing on tip-toe to dip prawny fingers into holy water

– genuflect while the organist strikes up something solemn,
thick, mottled hands trudging over keys, a slippered foot

pumping the pedal. At the appointed moment, a slow
procession up the cathedral's aisle to receive the holy bread

from Father – his sweat-fat face capillaried from one too many
bloods of Christ – moving in close for the transaction, each flat

dry disc stuck, then peeled off the roofs of mouths. Overhead,
the ceiling fans grind – keeping the sly heat of sin circulating.

In the days prior, on a trip to the Shrine gift-shop on Ruthven
Street, I browsed an assortment of sacrament-junk: painted

ceramic bible-vases and plastic statuettes of the Virgin Mary;
icons of saints and stained-glass keepsakes, everything,

emblazoned with the power of prayer. Nuns in neat blouses
gliding behind a silky oak counter, totting up sums with pencil-

licks; slipping purchases into paper bags. Somewhere, in a box
of old things, there's a class photograph of us all: hands pressed

together as if in prayer, all pious and pure – and you and me
at the back, wearing strings of rosary beads like Madonna.

"I am a good little girl.
I have pen and ink cause I am a good little girl…
I have got a red frock like my father.
Come here to see my father.
I have got sore feet and shoes and stockings and I am very glad."
Mathinna, 1842, Hobart Tasmania

Mathinna

And what do the towns-folk know of Mathinna, chieftan's daughter?
Her name hangs, centuries heavy, off the neck of a broken mining town
– a hopeless place given in to a thousand slow ways to drown.
Plucked from Wybalenna – taken on a whim of the Governor's wife.
Dressed up in fine colonial things: a native curios, spinning and spinning
in a picnic flock of white dresses on the grassy bank of the Derwent.

To cut open the black gut of the apple: drive deep into its gold-toothed
caverns, into the gaping sores left by generations of prospectors. These
are disappearing places – only good for raking over old headstones, for
understanding ancestral stories of one's own. On the outskirts of town
a pair of wild deer pick delicately across the road – slip seamlessly into
scrub, into badlands pocked with shafts and traps for miles around.

She clings to the edge of wildness – built and razed on the promise of
discovery; rounded up. Propped on a pedestal of ruin. Mathinna, quiet
in a red frock at the dinner table, Mathinna, asleep inside the Franklins'
realm. The threads of dreaming, spun thin to nothing. It's August, and
smoke signals wind wearily to the sky. Slack-jawed locals turn, follow
the car in, surprised by someone new. Jagged instincts crowd blood.

Mathinna is a town of things piled up. Car wrecks on car wrecks. Broken bits of fences, rubbish, metal things. Frontier woodpiles taller than a man. A well-kept graveyard curated with care, as if polite signs were enough to keep the tragedies of this place out. Quartz-crunch feet flattening the brittle bones of gold miners. On a corner block, a house crouches, gutted by fire: blackened limbs in twisted rigor mortis pose.

And what do they know of Mathinna, the great Towterer's daughter? Left to cultural purgatory when the Franklins sailed out – too white; not white enough, too black, too savage. Disappearing: a half-shadow of a woman, drinking herself to drowning. Her name hangs, centuries heavy, off the broken neck of an old mining town. In midday quiet, a pubescent girl holding a baby emerges on a porch, blinks clean the sun.

Across the road out of town, a thick black snake stretches out its length.

Time-share

In the threadbare dark, night is collecting in makeshift cups:
the gutters of this tinderbox; the visible parts of your body.

I lie awake, synchronising our breathing, night swimming across
a floral coverlet that has never suited you, or me.
                                           It's too hot for sleeping.

This suburban eucalypt tract is defined by species and sweat:
the brutal mating sounds of koalas tearing holes in the silence.
                                             The slow pulse of ecology.

We are as obvious: a peristaltic churn – coiling and uncoiling under
the skin of python weather, immediacy the only tangible bind.
                                             The only thing I can claim.

Outside, the night sky is decomposing – a familiar caveat:
first light over the departure gate, gut-black the colour of your going.

Farm Duties

She didn't look like she was having fun
when the drake surprised her,
thick yellow feet scrabbling,
slipping off her wings as he worked
her soft white feathers dramatic
against the startled green grass.
Tail whipping, beak nipping the back
of her head – as he braced against his
own carnal force. And when it was over,
she waddled slowly away. Shook out
her feathers. Drank long and deep from
the pond. Further distant, the drake met
another male bird as if in conversation.
They both fluffed out their wings.

The Instinct of Sharks

Go back to the start,
before the loneliness of two a.m. mating seasons carried you home:
   watch the bruise on your thigh shrink and disappear from your skin
   starve the sideshow alley clowns, take back the deal with the night

Go back to the start,
before the dance floor haze of your memory worked loose:
   lift the neon-soak from the dark and let the streetlights blink off
   cash in your chips, ignore the persuasion of sticky carpet

Go back to the start,
before the hammerhead light of morning burned the curtains:
   unstack and refill plastic cups, distinguish every face
   retrace your steps, save your judgement psalms for the unholy

Go back to the start,
before you crept out, drank tap-water from cupped hands:
   let the smell of liquor dry out and vanish from your dress
   hold everything together, keep your hand on your purse

Go back to the start,
before you stepped into the first terrible song of morning:
   cover your tenderised flesh and count out your small change
   remember how tired the glitter strip seems by day

Go back to the start,
before the last light turned off, and you forgot where your skin began:
   fold and unfold on repeat, breathe deeply in the back seat of a taxi
   remember the smell of blood, remember the instinct of sharks.

South Solitary

Solitude is a dark but simple art. It's easy, standing
here to imagine myself an island, exposed and obvious
laying darkly, quietly, waiting for coordinates, over-
looking this stretch of shipping death-waters.
I walk the headland's elbow to the continent's edge,
let squall-weather strip out the salt, the heat, each
carefully applied layer: I dissolve into abstracts,
unseen cells, matter tinier than the parts of breath.
The whip-lash of my hair, the heavy buffeting of my limbs
builds an updraft for flattened wings – brings me eye-
level with the rim of the ocean. I offer no resistance:
pulled and forced into a shape, a skin of human parts
arcing, folding: sucked through an unseen wall of thermal
drifts, dragging with me days of certain bad weather.
I tumble over the ageing bones of spooked vessels,
each resting, kindling-split, deep on the ocean's floor,
sleep-dreaming for decades under shifting salt-covers.
This is the wrecking season. I feel it: the sting of short,
dark days, the signal flares of circling shear-waters
over out-posted rookeries – the perfect way they
make parentheses around each anchor: each exposure
of personal desire, each soaring, tumbling thought –
hacked out at the root: capturing the wildness
that no lighthouse could ever predict.

Terrarium

January, and this place is dripping with snakes,
dusk-wings damp and pinned tight to spine's
contour, pressed flat by the buzz-saw weight of
cicadas; torpid heat – defeating the idea of exit.

I exist in this terrarium of my own making, tying
the same ends, again and again: letting the same
domestic scenes beat out. Hours west, a purpling
canvas builds, spews rumbling-wild alerts to run.

Sweat prickle beneath shrink-wrap compression,
the insufferable proximity of body parts: sex-swell
curves, the damp movement of back-flesh under
spaghetti straps, sticking points on every surface.

I imagine the laundry list I would leave for you: the
final shapes I'd impress: room-by-room, your finger-
tips on my objects, the smell of me, leaching from
bedlinen; the gun-fire battery of rain on the tin roof.

Ocean draws itself back into wildness. Beachside
parking meters hum and click out: the hard edge
of summer drawn in every shade of blue but cool,
concrete boxes menacing the sky into submission.

I imagine the aftermath: crisp light falling in bright
stripes on the bedroom floor, memory pulled clean
off the bone, a king parrot flashing across the dead-
sea sky. Over static: my voice, ringing out like a bell.

Home

All the doors are closed, as thin as paper.
The barrel slides – cold-clicked. Locked.
Every evening is a waiting game, scored in brutal harms.
In this existence, small change matters.
Documents, in hidden places. Somewhere distant,
the words of your mother. The clock ticks.
You're alert to incoming sounds – a closing car door,
the tell-tale crunch of leaf-litter. Outside,
the scalloped edges of the night exist gently, hung from
tenterhooks, deep and purpling.
The moon is pinned on, a communion wafer,
in a sky that's heard every confession. Where it starts
and where it ends is less obvious when you're drifting.
The same child, crouched low and lead-bellied,
is the same woman. A father's fists, working like a stamper-
battery, are the same young, angry hands.
Adrenaline prickles in the same way,
climbs a vertebrae ladder to the mind.
Entrenched normal flows from room to room.
In the drinking you started back then, to forget. In the dawn,
which appears mostly new, day after day after day.
A wearied-yellow bruise fading in the heat-haze
of Brisbane suburbs. Domestic details standing memory-bright.
Little smiles in picture frames. The tea-time things
scattered over the floorboards.
The daffodils he brought you last Monday, heads heavy,
lolling on softening stems. Know enough to ghost out.
Write clean the names of the survivors.
Tomorrow, the same moon lights a new kind of unknown.
Think. Don't think. The same door waits open.

II.
Tourniquet

"With my voice
I am calling you"
Nick Cave and the Bad Seeds, Jesus Alone

Wattlebird Pie

Stands of stringy-bark and blue gum at dawn
– the smell of blood-iron, close on the air's cold quiet.

Boy-marksman moving with intent: a bag of hessian
slung across his body – the warm death of wattlebirds

hanging like comfort at his back. Half-a-dozen, and
plump-enough – five or six birds to dignify a meal.

The old man's rifle: a job for both hands; 12-shot to
keep each carcass intact – gun-cracks spiking, then

spreading slow above the bush around Nine Mile Springs.
Daydreaming when the hammer fell, surprised him:

the guttural call of the wattlebird – a mimic for his
own desperate voice. The fine, floating substance of his

breath; blood leaching, warm and thick into damp leaf-
litter; the sudden mutilation of eye socket, cheek, lip.

His mother, back at the hut, fisting flour and mutton fat
on a board: the butcher's hook swinging empty.

A thin fowl appears at the door, scratching out of habit.
Further distant, the sound of an axe rings out. There's talk

in the camp of sinking a new shaft soon. The knuckles of
hunger pull through all of them, like beads on a rosary.

For Aylan Kurdi, who died in the Mediterranean Ocean on 2 September, 2015

Aylan

the sea offers up your name…the sea offers up your name
the sea offers up your name…the sea offers up your name
offers up your name, offers up your name, offers up your
name… your name, your name, your name, your name
the sea offers up your name…the sea offers up your name
the sea offers up your name…the sea offers up your name
your name, your name, your name, your name, your name
offers up your name, offers up your name, offers up your
name… your name, your name, your name, your name
the sea offers up your name…the sea offers up your name
the sea offers up your name…the sea offers up your name
offers you… offers you… offers you… offers you.. offers up
your name, your name, your name, your name, your name
your name, your name, your name, your name, your name
the sea offers up your name…the sea offers up your name
the sea, the sea, the sea, the sea, the sea, sea, sea, sea, sea

see.

Manus Island Love Poem

Simmer | Shimmer | Haze | Burn

Ya zamaa jaanukai...　　　　Oh my darling...
　　　　　this distance will not contain me.

　　　　Slow　　　**Slower**　　　**Slowest**

Click | Fizz | Wire | Cut

Place　　　**Displace**　　　　**Misplace**

　　　　　　　　　　　　　Forget | Forgotten

sabr wukra khodai ba de sha krri
　　　　be patient. God will do right by you.

　　Low　　　**Lower**　　　**Lowest**

Ignore | Ignite | Inflame

Blank　　　**Blanker**　　　**Blankest**

yesterday, a tree trunk exploded into knots
　　　　and I carved your name upon my body

Quiet | Disquiet

　　　Wire　　　**Wired**　　　**Heywire**

　　　　　　　Space | Between | Mirage

Wait. Waiting

bakhshana ghuarrum　　　　　Forgive me.

Long**Longer****Longest**

Fence | Difference
_____

_____**Differences**

Bake | Broil | Burn

Silence. Silent.

za ta der yadawom…I miss you so much…

Hard**Harder****Hardest**

Rage | Cry | Sleep

Breathe. Breathing

bakhk'hena ghwaarremI'm sorry…

I feel you, now, here next to me.

Small**Smaller****Smallest**

Dead | Empty | Nothing

Drowned.

Drowned.

Drowned.

Forgive me…habiib albi

za la ta sara meena kawom

I will always love you.

Bellarine Machines

Escape.
A sparkling sash of sand, wiped clean:
    a lemon-pale transfusion
    dawning over the head

Norfolk pines rim the bay,
loose in relaxation pose:
    the city's breath burned-up
    by the first phase of the sun

Bellarine machines come and go,
micro-domiciles in sunset-coloured racing stripes:
    drop orderly anchors,
      leave nothing behind

It's the coming back
that we have grown good at,
    building our houses of cards:
    consumerist messes of rigs
    and swimming towel bunting

We run to water
to see how far we have fallen short,
    find rolling baptism
    in coke bottle-backed waves

Across the park,
besser bricks cast sunshine patterns
    on apocalyptic bedfellows,
    as we strike out,
      greet something hard and pure

Behind our backs, the sky keeps building,
a meringue-soft levee, holding back the tide:
    that grey and familiar load
    tumbling again

        and again

over the break.

Pristella Maxillaris

There's a man, dead, not far from the concrete ankles
of the housing commission towers

slack-mouthed boxes, blunt cut against every kind of sky
with no design on reaching, or being reached

generational stain – even the stairwells are sick with it
inside, pillbox pensioners wither on the vine.

In these uncertain, early hours, there's no short-cut through here.

He's lain prone for hours now – the awkwardness of corduroy
married perfectly to his vanishing point, to dawn shallows.

Brunswick Street is a dark jewel: *Pristella Maxillaris* –
a luminous splint holding up suburban fragments.

Terraces in working class suits claim the city end,
peeled back and examined for vital signs, as tramlines

feed the strip – a slow-moving tourniquet, squeezing out
what's left of the bleeding hearts.

It's all vintage, you know.

Last Easter, a Jesuit came to wash the feet of men like him,
reflect on the idea of restoration.

This morning, day breaks no differently than before – outside,
the same pigeon-wing sky is flooding, drinking itself to death.

There's a man, laying dead, not far from here.

Break-up

the night we broke
we laid a blood-spiked substrate
of constellation shards
and domestic instruments

I found myself,
alone in a crowded quiet
on the kitchen floor
accepting gravity
and imperfection:
a slice of toast
gone cold in the slots,
the arrhythmic wheeze
of whitegoods

the clock's tick –
an anvil-struck hurt

every space – too big
for an aftermath like this

Climbing Mount Yasur

Rising from the Tannese jungle: the early evening flicker of free-
range villages. All thatch and weave – pinched back from Cyclone
Pam's great churn, from the dried-out limbs of dead palm trees.

I'm in an off-road convoy to Yasur, watching light fail from electric
to pin-prick to nothing, fire-smoke curling to the darkened hangar
of the cargo gods, an address book for even the unkindest of weather.

The old woman rises to the north, blowing her stack over and over,
Pacific winds whipping her breath out to the warming, rising sea.
Roughed up, I'm 4-wheel drive loose, and not of my own body.

We ascend, a conga-line of phone-clutching tourists - momentary,
each grey ash footprint just deep enough to cradle the next. The
hot wind rushes the moonscape like a grit-spiked battering ram.

Belly-rumble-spit – the old woman coughs up orange confetti,
fuelled by sulphur-steam and the boom-shake of dragons' feet.
Compelled, I'm lost in infernal rage, ash floor quaking beneath me.

One wrong move, the thought pulsing sharp behind my eyes.
One wrong move, my body a spinning husk – burning up like paper.
The earth bursts forth again and again, shakes its fist at all of us.

Signs of life

Below the port-facing ribs of the old town
the body of the St Lawrence River is laid out

October clears the decks, blows the last of the tourists
down the creases of the Vieux Montreal

In stone-walled urban pockets, spot fires burn
with the suddenness of maple leaves,

an ox-blood undertow, turning slowly to face the fall

I am glowing from the inside too, but
with a migrational pull that is much less seasonal

barely noticeable under grey-marbled sky,
a gentle drift of ashes with no shaft of light for reveal

How strange that I keep finding myself here,
lost in a crush of North American monuments

navigating unexpected points of cultural difference
and icebox doors weighted against winter's shoulder

Small, unfamiliar birds are fleeing this place
and each flight pattern catches like something intimate

When I return to my body, the city continues, as all cities do
the towering heartlands of vacant gods growing closer

Even here, inside the Basilica on Rue St Sulpice
comfort is temporary, a sub judice resting place

for my own turning chrysalis

Inside the emptiness of noise, the acoustics are perfect
for a new heartbeat, I can't hear yet.

Homesick on the Plateau Mont-Royal, Montreal

On the commercial skin of the Plateau Mont-Royal
graffiti-bricked cafés are the city's laughed-in lines

I have come here, with culturally sound intentions, to
try the local delicacy – the *poutine* of cheese curds and fries

the baby can't kick yet, but I am sick and craving home comforts:
blue sky dreaming – the *crick, crick, crick,* of summer's creep

how I wear it, even here – an ecological timepiece.

My schoolgirl French has slipped away like a fistful of tugging
balloon strings, and I find myself, existing against the grain

wanting the romance of the Quartier Latin, but in this tug-of-war city
linguistics are serious, and English apostrophes are outlawed.

Here, I feel stripped back to something raw, so for now, sign language
suits me just fine – café au lait and croissants are just fine

soon, every decision will be hamstrung by time.

Balloon

The blue marble of mother's milk
is a roadmap to your half-filled tomb

– an absent bloodline, orphaned
on the vast embrace of your chest

you are awake inside your sleep
curled small among the sheets; still

luminous – somewhere under your
flatline and all the visible bruises

and this sudden ferocity that fills
our shared emptiness, has teeth and

muscle, it strikes out lost intentions
– silences the death of black swans

tonight, there is something sacred
about the contours of your body:

the wishbone glow of your ankles
in the moon's bathwater,

the velvet ripple of your abdomen,
as your tide carries away the last boat

nothing is as shapeless as this night
or the ones that will follow it

in the early morning light,
I will still be here, picking through

tired chrysanthemum heads –
wiping the milky way from your skin

Something Old, Something New

After dusk, there are fewer things of beauty. The sky has shifted,
painted itself into a corner – called in a strange weather.

All the satellites we know are in shadow and instinct has taken
over. I am inside this, driving to the mother of your children's

house – sweeping through domestic flotsam, patient as a sonar.
The streetlights are in flood, thick with the winged static

of insects and flight paths, each moving somewhere – searching
for a way in, or maybe a way out. And with unconscious hands

I unhook the hurt, draw tight the neck of its bag – to conceal
the barbs and traps I have assembled inside.

This is still enemy territory.

I'm not yet divorced from this scene – I have grown solid inside
the thought of it, gear-change smooth and barely raising a ripple.

Outfoxing curiosity for months after households changed hands,
pouring effortlessly into the spaces you left behind, my clothes on

your hanging rails – my body asleep beside your husband's.
I give you nothing, even now as you open the door – spoiled by

your own hand – camp-drafted clean from the mob and pulled apart
by your own impulsive horses. Inside this haunting you have created

I can hardly see you – a slip-stitched mess of dark pieces; limbs and
obvious bones. A slow-moving weather system under your skin.

The night is holding, for now. From your bedroom window, a white curtain unfurls its length as the night breathes out the charges

against you. They crash, crippled and spared of wings at your feet, and I wonder if this is it —

    if this is what winning looks like.

Toowoomba Carnival Queen

Shacked up
with camphor laurel brutes

the carnival queen
exhausts volcanic soil:

> rising damp
> and a pair of knuckle-bark thighs,

a name,
scrawled across a postcard

> of sweet, blue violets

did you know her
in those unsealed moments
before dawn opened up?

fogged in
at the range crossing:

> listening for the Angelus bells?

this city
is as famous for its murders, as its flowers

for the splinters
that didn't work their way out

September is coming:

> coaxed by conservative hands
> in sensible gardening gloves

across the escarpment,
jacaranda trees are starting to snow.

The Hazards #1

End of day. Mottled daylight and empty oyster shells.
The Hazards: a grey-pink jaw closing around the bay.

Night begins its advance – a sable-smooth awning
pulling slowly over the two of us, dark and familiar.

Our silence is an albatross: exposing the gentle music
of masts, drifting in night-chill shadows. Seclusion

snaps the distance between us like a snare drum.
Tramontane wastelands peel back, reveal ligaments.

My hand finds yours and I read you like a telegram:
how strange that this dialect of comfort remains,

even when darkness spills over into blood.
Soon, the last of the birds will fall as silent as death.

The Hazards #2

I am smaller here, beside you
under the weight of the sky.

The bay has rejected my echo,
released all the gulls – and

the sounds of the gloaming
are suddenly giant.

In this slender bridge of day
between bruised hours

I'm hanging out our shapes
with precision and cold hands

moving domestic chess pieces,
slowly giving myself away.

Evandale

The broken bits of this town
        have been painted over.
Behind the village strip, life crouches
inside a slow ruin.

Tourists roll on and through,
take breakfasts of warm bread and eggs
inside squat English-style boxes.
I came here to be someone else,
paint out the damage
        imagine I am whole.

A pearl-rimmed sky
        rings morning's arrival.
The bees hang over the daisies.
The starlings press in with an
        incessant chirrup-song
Their tiny avian hammers
        Beating
        Beating

By evening,
I imagine them, thick and tumbling
from my pockets, my ears
        the sockets of my eyes
scissoring their way
with their beaks under my flesh.
        Thinking is impossible.

So I walk,
through the 19th century
    brick work of this town
waiting for nightfall,
for an internal silence.

Everything is postcard-pretty:
    the late sun, striping through the arbour
    the smell of wood-smoke,
a crate of apples inside a shop window
a gang of silky hens wandering loose

Everything is arranged just so,
watercolour soft and beautiful,
the way Glover would have painted it

I skim across this canvas,
until nightfall drags along sleep:
    and even then,
      there's no pigment deep enough
      to paint it out –
the same small town darkness that runs
through me,
    through the people living here, streets-deep.

III.
Occlusion

"One man wasting another man
One hand washes the other hand"
Jerry Cantrell, Dickeye

Skin

How small the spaces
between each individual act   of erosion
How absent the worn-out parts of the body
you   forgot how to love

Water from the kettle
for the slough and sluice of cells   clean off you
ring-barked   skin, stains in the tub
the slow strip of tenancy

Imagine the parts of you washed
down to the creek, maybe even far to the sea
How small, the effort between ebb and   surrender
the way you draw yourself back

How vast, the idea that breath   alone
could shift a landscape, leave you
to grow fat inside a still   life of your own making
carve out your colours with a knife

For Frederick Fidgett Fiddaman who died 4 June 1882

A Remittance Man

Was it some kind of darkness or idiocy
that saw him shipped off to a colony where he'd be less bother,
undesirable-black sheep-dissolute-drunken-ne-er-do-well
a convict without chains, paid to stay away: scratch-eke-scrap.
Even his name some kind of joke: Frederick Fidgett Fiddaman
a remittance man – of an arrangement sat below the poverty line
to keep the family shame-embarrassment-disgrace distant:
swapping London for a lucky strike existence on the creeks
and headlands of Gumbaynggirr country, hacking rough-as-guts
mine shafts and shitting out mullock heaps.

His drowned body rests beneath the local caravan park office:
buried a pauper-hermit at his unfortunate end –
I imagine he'd have hated the fact his name attached itself to this
stretch of cashed-up north coast with its luxury homes, and
flash women in designer linen shirts walking delicate dogs;
he'd have hated the fact his name marks the road and creek here,
the fact the beach named for him stretches on like a gold seam.
A remittance man – sold off to the arse end of the world,
forever solid on the tongues of new money in their glass houses:
million-dollar views through every soaring window.

Keilawarra

She was lost in a big year for shipwrecks,
to the deep waters somewhere off North Solitary Island
punctured, rolled, then sucked aft-first, perpendicular
and sunk fathoms under the dark ocean –
it was more than a century before she was found again by divers.

That night, the whole terror lasted seven minutes,
the length of screams, the powerful suction
enough time for the best and worst of humanity, the panic – revealed
in the gendered ratio of death, every man for himself
second class objects left bobbing on the dark surface of the ocean.

And when the steamer's dying sounds
were erased from the night, a list was made of thirty-five survivors
just two women, both named Alice, making it out
– one clung to a box; another to a bag of chaff:
did they go on, raise fire-brand daughters?

Newspapers reported a couple of bodies washed ashore,
one with a sandy-whiskered face, one wearing printed trousers
and a blue striped shirt
more common were the cargo treasures that washed up:
a crate of cucumbers, 24 cases of tallow, some of golden syrup.

And what of the racehorse mare *Fidelity?*
carefully loaded by the stevedores back in Sydney, packed in
with a box of bees, buggy parts, and a prize heifer
there's a story she swam ashore that night
ran wild for years in the bush around Coffs Harbour

– died on her own terms, of natural causes.

Fontanelle

Midday beats on Brewarrina. Everywhere, the dead art
of sign writing marks a portal to another misplaced place.

Drifters are crouched outside the roadhouse, face-deep
in itinerant shadow – the slow slap of rubber thongs on tar

measuring time's movement. In the Gamba grass, decades
of wasteland spoil are buried with the message sticks.

There's something dangerous about the middle distance,
in the quiet menace of scarecrow men – kerosene eyes

that swim beyond social convention. Out here, heat is not
the only mirror that exposes the dark heart pumping away

inside all of us. Grey nomads pass through town, pressing
the auto-locks – fumbling with maps. This is our existential

blind spot – without words but not unspoken; a shared
endlessness, still littered with the same dingo fences.

Maranoa

i
Morven blood moon
he stares down
at a plate of something fried

ii
outside Mungallala
two young boys
sever a wallaby's tail

iii
high noon
the sun strikes the river
like rifle fire

Itinerant Damnation #1

Arrival: another moth-eaten sunset town,
another routine work around.

Outside the car, he sweats down the backs of his legs
– feels exposed.

Near the fisho, a crow picks at something crook-necked,
and it stirs something primal inside his own blood.

The snap of bone,
that young bloke's arm bloody and useless,
– his sudden look of surprise and terror.

It follows him here.

This town feels the same as the one before,
and he fashions for it a familiar skin.
Picks laundromat coins from the car seats
later on, takes a glass of something hard and a Chinese meal.

He's alone,
works the lazy susan with knuckle-blown hands,
listens to the slack sounds of his own mouth.

Red silk lanterns remind him of distance –
of the unknown miles it takes to outrun the dead.

And after tablecloth vinyl has been wiped clean of him
he leaves replaceable parts of his body on motel room sheets.

Waits it out. Another town,
another useless crescent moon.

Itinerant Damnation #2

He returned to Opalton to check for bones.
Treading rust over abandoned mine shafts – over blind scars
left by men like him: brutes that hacked and raped.

Not much speaks of survival now but the crow, pitch-eyed
and scanning for death. The tea-stained saltbush steeps.
Carcasses are pinned to the earth where they dropped.

Some things remain, call out the vacancy in creeping shadows.
The shoulders of an old hut – its eyes and mouth punched in.
The honest inheritance of light.

Over there, was where he killed a man,
his young, foolish ribs driven deep into the ridge like nails.
The arms of the brigalow reach up, clawing like hell against the sky.

Unpicking the seams is easy, when the luck of a desperate man
has burned out. This whole place is held together by luck.
Desiccated shapes and rotted skeletons,

all of it, waiting its turn for dust. He scuffs about, smokes.
Works the red dirt out from under his fingernails with a knife.
Turns his horse's head for the north.

For Evelyn, Elizabeth and Janet

The Torpey Spoon

Home is the colour of sunlight through the kitchen window,
a lemon-curd glow, filled thick with floating dust motes.

I'm inside with my young daughter, crafting a version of love
from cooling figs and a row of gingham-capped jars.

And with each turn of our old cooking spoon, I'm borrowing
maternal lore; making simple transactions of inheritance.

Some household relics endure in the retelling, become
the glory box gifts worth leaving – like this simple spoon

placed by my grandmother's hands and her mother's before
hers, deep in a calico-lined tea chest. The kind of old spoon

that carried the heart of a kitchen. Wide-mouthed and generous,
with lipped edges that could curl snug around a single egg

or stir resilience through with service when the winds changed.
During weeks that stretched to months when the creek dried up,

when tall, brown beer bottles kept an empty meat-safe company;
when something could always be made from nothing.

A domestic instrument with a defined use and a dozen undefined
others; a generational orphan, an extension of matriarchal hands.

This afternoon, we measure distance together, making jam and
history, ghosted by the thickening fingers of bush brides.

And as Saturday floats, I am witness to my daughter's
industry, working beside me with small, deliberate hands.

Day slides away and crickets crowd the night air with an earthly
thrum. From the back steps, the sky turns the colour of eternity.

The Mort Street Badlands

Beneath the paling-slatted skirt of his grandmother's house
was a strange, striped world of uncertain light
       a curious space between floorboards and drought-stamped soil
          where everything seemed unfinished

A dumping ground for the whims of long-gone children
the metal husks of machines and bicycle bits grown grey and bearded

A half-hearted containment line for rabbit holes and shadowlands
     where the dust light would float,
          dervish-beautiful along the lengthening arms of winter

The place where darknesses boiled up, with a physicality
that drew you in

As a child, he kept his secrets here too, folded carefully
inside Capstan tins, hidden up high on white-ant caps
– during the holiday weeks that bled through the loneliness
    into his child's eye,
        truth hanging loose inside his memory box

Sometimes, he'd wait behind the laundry door,
until his feet turned numb against the concrete slab
– watching for her to enter, split firewood for the woodstove

Listening for the *thump, thump* and *crack* –his breath small as she swung
the axe, throwing her shoulder, again and again:
     lost, somewhere violent, inside pensioner floral
         a snow-white lock of her hair working loose

In those moments, she had the body of a stranger – no longer
grandmother, but stick-thin firebrand; young,
        before she was wrung out over bitter nights
                a kerosene lamp swinging inside the blackness

It was always the dark that thrilled him most – its claw and pick,
the sudden way it would unfold in the corners he kept close
exploding, flint-strike hot against the skulls of small creatures
        gut-deep, here in these badlands
                somewhere between instinct and everything else.

Petrichor

Travelling west – it's easy to forget the petrichor of rain
        much harder, the effortless pressure of your hands

heat sleeps in stalactites from small town pickets:
        from garden furniture – a mess of leaning skeletons,
        phalanges straining in the dust bowl

out here – it's easier
to admit a loss of direction:
        it began much further south than this

I was a young man in that moment – when distance
began to mean more than a half-closed door, and
        now, kilometres from my everywhere
        and I'm no closer to anything you ever told me

each day is an artefact, fixed at noon
caught somewhere between history and the highway

this border town gives nothing away:
        stuffs its secrets in the back pockets of patriarchal whites
        as another cruel summer curls the laminate

There's nothing of myself to leave behind here.

Tyenna: *What comes after extinction*

The valley ribbons west along the Derwent,
a sweet-spot of green pasture – fat with the caramel
flanks of cows and the symmetry of orchards
– a picture of cool-climate fruiting country.
It's too early for cherries, and the hops are slow
to stir beside high-wire trellises.
Oast houses dot village cheeks,
standing damp and vacant as spring leans in,
the white arms of maybushes aching along the highway.

Tyenna is a post script now, mapped
beyond this quiet country –
whittled thin in the shadow of alpine reaches.
Where Mount Mawson's breath travels just far enough
to anoint the visible parts of flesh,
to signal the strengthening hold of the wild.
All but gone, save for a few tired holdings,
an unkept pioneer graveyard.

When the sawmills and bullock teams
stopped, bushfires took the rest – frontier histories
dissolving on the burning tongues of custodial spirits.

The wildness crept back by increment,
the choking cold of the river, thick
with immigrant species – the mountains and their
hidden places, the heaviness of untamed things.
One hundred years ago, the last thylacine
was seen alive near here, perhaps too the last dead.
Maybe this town was always meant for
extinction – for country to take back.
Below the surface, no one notices the survivors.
The speckled bodies of river trout multiply,
weaving in unintelligible formations.

In February 1843, Stanton House, at Back River near New Norfolk, was robbed by bushranger Martin Cash and his gang.

Back River

There's an electric fence to keep the cow out of the orchard,
but she pays no mind. Moves her taupe-velvet
bulk with purpose through the promised land.
What she desires, she will take.
The hills of Magra rise to the east, where sheep
have gathered under the old macrocarpa tree.
This is bushranging country, vantage-rich.
I can feel the early distance of this place,
drum-tight days — all those maddening months
between visitors.
Inside, the sunlight is filtered and warm,
flooding up sandstone stairs to this aspect.
I've forgotten that it's Sunday today,
and colonial thoughts summon something calm.
There's a certain reassurance to the history
of a place — to the handsome bones of this house,
or the way Back River acreage still lingers.
Fat green paddocks with scrubby walls.
The sounds of animals before humans —
the distant tap of a shoe striking floorboards.
Somewhere in these same hills,
is the hide-out where Cash and his gang watched,
waiting for their chance at this place.
I imagine the household stuffed inside
the drawing room: the ladies languid,
 — begging for something to happen.

On 24 January 2015 Lefroy's avenue of honour was rededicated, and a memorial installed alongside three remaining 'soldier trees'.

Soldier Trees

Stirring south, on the edge of an island-state winter – a
flesh-burn cold meets the ANZAC dawn. Days begin as they
end, melting slowly over back roads where Lefroy sleeps,
a half-light town of vacant blocks and great-war ghosts.

The early mist lifts in patches, reveals the hearth-plumes
of distant households, unfurling like standards to greet the sky.
Packets of sheep have been shaken out over paddocks
– where the light pools, saucer-deep.

Seasonal reefs carve across lemon-gold hills of gorse,
soft against a more distant purple. Rust-tipped shrubs
follow watercourses, winding through old prospecting
country – quick, dirty wealth pumping alluvial veins.

The road carves through this pastoral idyll,
gives way to scrub, and back again. Less travelled now,
and thick with wattlebirds, with only shadow-lines
and soldier trees left to tell of the retreat.

One hundred years ago, eleven oaks were planted here
for the local boys left cold on the Western Front –
a ceremonial shovel was brought in for the job:
bayonet-heavy in the gloved hands of young widows.

Soldier trees, watching over the slow slip away to ruin.
When the post office closed its doors, buildings
worth saving were carried away north to Beaconsfield.
No shaft could be sunk deep enough to slow the death.

You can imagine this place by studying its bones: a
bitumen grid framing up nothing, a clutch of junkyard
houses – dug in on a disappeared main street, a neat
bus shelter, stapled to an empty corner block.

From every vantage point, memorials to death;
and an Australian flag, flying from a freshly painted white pole.

Inheritance

i

There's a complex certainty in coming home.
It keeps on, something like faith – shakes the red dirt
shoulders of the Maranoa and prickles up a spine

of Ooline trees to the west. I have not travelled nine
hours here bearing sorry words, because this poem
has long been carved into the palms of my hands.

This is not the place for absolution. Not here, where
clay plains repeat with the smell of ashes and burning.
This is a wasteland for sepia-drenched stiffs, and crows

tossing gunfire emptiness with bullet-point eyes. I'd
rather drive through this molasses-thick heat, away from
ancestral fossils. Out here, Mandandanji feet know the earth

and I am only a stranger – a tightly clenched prodigal
alone with the pull of regret behind my rib cage.
Out of the car, I fall hard into my own body.

ii

There's a fanfare building in the mess of my chest,
at first – the dull insignificance of white noise, a bedrock
for more obvious sounds. Ghost movements about the old

homestead's bones as daylight's axe splits the dawn.
A tin mug, filled rough from the bore – a timpani
to ring out a father's cut-throat kind of loving. Cattlemen

have such little cause for conversation and I never knew
how this land could colour your blood, ink your
shadow. How it could spark like live wires across the

fence post props of this old town; mouth dropped down
at one side – beaten to chalk dust by heat. Still, a strange
beauty glows in small town geography. And even here

by Oolandilla Creek (where nothing is particularly beautiful)
something bigger burns through me – leaves white light and
saltbush scars, my fingers moving along the same lines as yours.

iii
At the back of the cemetery, I sit by you, wearing cobblers' pegs
and eating plums from the Amby store – wondering if your
constant absence was just your version of a blessing.

But it's easier to understand all this out here, when the land
continues before you've even noticed it begin; the quiet flow of
the Maranoa River pushing on, emptying slowly into the Balonne.

At the artesian spa in town, a trio of boys hold a fourth
under water, til he thrashes like a hessian-bagged red-belly.
There's not a soul in Cambridge Street after midday, as a

B-double truck rumbles over the bridge. From a clutch of
belah trees, a black-striped wallaby appears, turns to outback
coral then dust. I think of your headstone, weathered to ghost

text and about the blinding nature of recall and bloodlines;
about how the walls of this dam always seem to hold, even when
the avalanche comes – and there is nothing else left but bones.

www.ingramcontent.com/pod-product-compliance
Lightning Source LLC
Chambersburg PA
CBHW020107240426
43661CB00002B/62